EN'S
RAT

WOMEN'S
AID SAYS NO
TO CORRIE
ANTI-
ABORTION
BILL

WOMEN'S
AID SAYS NO
TO CORRIE
ANTI-
ABORTION
BILL

PERKINS

ACKNOWLEDGEMENTS

Special thanks to all at Bookmarks for "minding the shop" while I wrote this and for the tremendous comradeship of the last eight years.

Thanks also to Christophe Chataigne, Noel Douglas, Mary Phillips, Pete Robinson and Patrick Ward for help with design and production.

Emma Bircham, Hannah Dee, Lindsey German, Anna Gluckstein, Chris Harman and Mark Thomas all made time to give comments, ideas and much encouragement, so a big thank you to them and to Martin Smith for all that and so much more.

ABOUT THE AUTHOR

Judith Orr is editor of Socialist Review magazine (www.socialistreview.org.uk)
judithorr@hotmail.com

INSIDE FRONT PHOTOGRAPH

TUC demonstration against the anti-abortion Corrie Bill in 1979.

INSIDE BACK PHOTOGRAPH

Women enter the factories in World War Two.

SEXISM AND THE SYSTEM: A REBEL'S GUIDE TO WOMEN'S LIBERATION - JUDITH ORR
PUBLISHED BY BOOKMARKS PUBLICATIONS 2007
10 DIGIT ISBN: 1905192231
13 DIGIT ISBN: 9781905192236
DESIGNED BY NOEL DOUGLAS (noel@noeldouglas.net)
PRINTED BY CAMBRIDGE PRINTING

women are defined as sex objects; porn, in the guise of lads' magazines, has come off the top shelf and is being read in the train seat beside you; and pole dancing is marketed as a great way for women to keep fit.

Many of those angry about the situation of women today call themselves feminists. There may be no single mass organisation of feminists in Britain today but generally the main feature of feminist politics is to argue that all women in society have a common bond around which we need to unite to fight for our rights. For some this logic can lead to seeing men as the main problem, with an interest in keeping women down.

But for many women this approach is not enough. For those who don't believe that all men are the enemy, or believe that not all women suffer equally, there is another political tradition, one that doesn't seek to pit women and men against each other, but argues instead that the majority of women and men have a mutual interest in changing the world.

This is the socialist tradition and it has something unique to say about the roots of women's oppression and how we can fight for a different society. We don't think women's place in society is natural, nor is it inevitable. We draw on a rich seam of socialist ideas on the politics of women's oppression going back to the 19th century. German revolutionary socialist Clara Zetkin, for example, wrote extensively on the question of women's liberation and was the first to propose and establish the 8th of March as International Women's Day, in 1910. It was the date that women garment workers had protested in New York two years previously in their campaign for the vote and better working conditions.

Sexism and the System

A Rebel's Guide to Women's Liberation

JUDITH ORR

★ Introduction

Today women are constantly being t[...] have it all". We can combine careers [...] children; we can become lawyers a[...] and even prime minister. There are laws to la[...] rights for maternity leave, equal pay and ag[...] harassment. What more could we want?

In fact some say that women's equality [...] too far, that women's success has meant th[...] emasculated, that their traditional jobs and [...] been eroded. We are told that that we now nee[...] about boys' achievment in school, implying [...] that girls have got better opportunities it mus[...] expense of boys.

But women are far from having it all. W[...] paid less than men and still carry the respon[...] most of the work in the home. New Labour's [...] market and addiction to feeding the needs o[...] ness have had a massive impact on the lives [...] class women who carry the major burden of [...] and social welfare cuts.

Women are also facing a seemingly u[...] barrage of raw sexism which is seeping int[...] of society. Writer Ariel Levy has called this d[...] "raunch culture" and for many young wom[...] is how the harsh reality of women's oppress[...] (Ariel Levy, *Female Chauvinist Pigs*, Pocket [...] They are angry about growing up in a [...]

don't believe in feminist

Women in the work force.

Those New York garment workers are also part of our tradition, for ever since women have been part of the workforce they have fought for better conditions, for equality and for justice. Such struggles continue to this day: the biggest ever strike of women workers in Britain took place in March 2006 over pension rights.

They are all part of an inspiring history of women and men fighting for women's rights like equal pay, education and access to abortion, but for so much more as well, for a society which sees the emancipation of all humanity.

This, then, is the socialist case for how we can fight for women's liberation.

★ 1. Can Marxism explain women's oppression?

Theories about the roots of women's oppression, or about gender differences in modern society, are often not much more than the mystical "women are from Venus, men from Mars" view under a different guise. The book of that name became a best seller ten years ago with its message that the only way men and women could get along was by imagining they came from two different planets (John Gray, *Men are from Mars, Women are from Venus: how to get what you want in relationships*, HarperCollins, 2002).

This popular approach to gender asumes that there are certain innate differences in attributes between women and men, for example:

* Women are caring, nurturing, cooperative and intuitive
* Men are aggressive, competitive and rational

These characteristics are said to be rooted in our biology, have been for all time and will never be any different. Therefore our different roles in society, and women's inferior position, are merely a reflection of that unchanging human nature.

One recent book on feminism even tried to explain

the Iraq war in terms of men's inherent testosterone-fuelled aggression. "The attacks of 9/11, the bombing of Afghanistan, the assault on Iraq and the 'war against terrorism', the ongoing cycle of violence between the Israeli army and the suicide-bombers, have all served to highlight the violence that prevails in a world ruled by an aggressive patriarchy" (Peggy Antrobus, *The Global Women's Movement*, Zed, 2004). This is a common refrain when it comes to explanations about war.

But it simply doesn't stand up to the facts. If war and soldiering are so natural for men, why do governments have to psych them up so much for battle and break them down in brutal boot camps? Why do so many serving soldiers in conflicts suffer serious psychiatric disorders, in some cases even leading them to suicide, caused by their experience of war? To say that aggression and war come easily to young men is an insult and lets the real warmongers off the hook. What do you say about Condoleezza Rice if you have this biologically determinant view of gender?

For women are not necessarily by nature meek and benign. Figures for bullying in schools for instance show that girls bully more than boys, and figures for child abuse show that mothers are as likely to abuse their children through violence or neglect, as are men in the family.

So this view of the world is just not good enough. It is impressionistic; it regards the prevailing ideas and structures in modern capitalism as if they are timeless unchanging characteristics of the human race. All it shows is how ideas about women and men have become part of the everyday common sense of today's society, even among some of those who say they want to challenge the system.

Marxism and oppression

Socialists have a very different approach. We don't think that just because women are second class citizens in every society across the world there must be something in our human nature that makes that inevitable. In fact for socialists women's liberation is central to our vision of a different society. If in any society women are still discriminated against, then it's not socialism, we haven't got there yet—it's as simple as that.

Yet we are often told that Marxism is economistic, that it is solely concerned with matters of economics, exploitation and wages, and is neither interested in nor able to explain women's oppression. Oppression, so the story goes, is "outside the economic model", and therefore can't be explained by an analysis of capitalism.

So can a theory based on the fact that class division is central to how society is organised explain oppression, something which cuts across all classes?

The answer is that Marxism is not the restricted set of ideas of the caricature. In fact Marx himself used the term "political economy", precisely because he saw his ideas not as narrowly dealing with economics but as a way of looking at and understanding every aspect of society.

Of course oppression cannot be reduced to class. All women in society suffer some form of oppression. You just have to look at how high earning women in the City are treated by male colleagues where there have been numerous high profile cases of sexual discrimination.

In one case investment bank Dresdner Kleinwort Wasserstein was sued for nearly £800 million by six female employees in New York saying they were treated as second class citizens despite many years of service.

Katherine Smith, from DKW's London office, said she was referred to as "the Pamela Anderson of trading" and another told of being pressured to leave a meal celebrating a business deal so her male colleagues could go to a strip club, while a third claimed that salesmen in her department said they hired females in junior positions because they wanted "eye candy".

On top of this treatment women in these top jobs are routinely ignored for promotion and paid less both in salaries and bonuses than men in the same positions. It may be difficult to empathise with women on six figure salaries with lifestyles to match, but the fact is what they are experiencing is a consequence of women's oppression.

Ruling class women are also trivialised when they are treated as trophies of rich men: having a glamorous young woman on your arm decked out in jewels and haute couture becomes just another flamboyant accessory like a flash car.

But to acknowledge that oppression can affect women in all parts of society does not mean that the experience of oppression is identical for all women. The experience of a trophy woman in a large house with nannies and cleaners and a chauffeur-driven car is very different to that of a woman working in a call centre with three children in a two bedroom council flat.

The role that exploitation plays means that women in the working class are more locked in by their oppression than women of the ruling class who, because of their class position, have more ability to overcome the practical difficulties facing them because of their gender. They have more economic independence to get out of a bad relationship, pay for childcare, have regular holidays, live in decent housing, to not have to cook every night. These options can ameliorate much of the very real burden that the majority of women carry every day.

So you cannot understand oppression by seeing it as something which runs parallel but separate to class exploitation, affecting all women equally. Instead oppression is inextricably entwined with wider class relationships. To deny the sometimes dramatic differences between women's lives, to look at oppression without acknowledging the impact of class, both belittles it and affects how you fight it. For women in the ruling class have an interest in maintaining the situation. They may suffer oppression but they also benefit from a state of affairs where the working class is passive and divided and where working class women accept low pay. So ruling class women will not be part of a fight to challenge the system.

A Marxist explanation of women's oppression begins from the fact that there is nothing "natural" either about the way we live today, or about what we think about each other and the world. And in terms of human history, class society and, even more so, modern capitalism are relatively recent forms of organisation. For the vast majority of human history there were no class divisions and women's oppression did not exist.

The following chapters will look at how women's oppression developed with the rise of class society and at how ideas about our world in general and about women in particular flow from the different ways society has been organised. This then offers a way forward to fighting for and winning a society free from oppression.

★ 2. Ideas do not fall from heaven, nothing comes to us in a dream*

Today many deeply sexist ideas about women persist. Women are judged by their looks and adult women are infantilised by being referred to as girls. In 2005 Lawrence H Summers, the then president of Harvard, one of the US's most prestigious universities, pronounced that there were few leading women in science as perhaps women were not hard wired for the subject. He was forced to retire early, and, with a nod to natural justice, has been replaced by the first woman president in the university's 371-year history, Drew Gilpin Faust.

Double standards about men and women's behaviour permeate popular opinion.

When an older man becomes a father he is the subject of admiring banter; when a woman does the same she is attacked for challenging nature for selfish ends. But when a 62-year-old British woman, Dr Rashbrook, became pregnant after in vitro fertilisation her doctor's comments only compounded society's sexist assumptions. Doctor Severino Antinori announced that he had treated her because "she is slim, blonde and in perfect condition, she fits all the criteria for maternity" (*Guardian*, 5 May 2006).

*Antonio Labriola, *Essays on the Materialist Concept of History*, Charles H Kerr, 1908

He was not asked if he would have treated her if she did not highlight her hair.

Every day brings new examples of sexist ideas, but what do we mean when we say that these ideas about expectations merely reflect our deeply unequal society, rather than cause it?

It means we are materialists, so we believe the real material world that we are born into, its structures and forms of social organisation, shapes the ideas in our heads. This is what Karl Marx meant with his often-quoted phrase, "Life is not determined by consciousness, but consciousness by life" (Karl Marx and Frederick Engels, *The German Ideology*, Lawrence and Wishart, 1970, p47).

This doesn't mean that socialists believe ideas are not important. On the contrary, it is vital that we challenge bigotry, whether it is sexism, racism or homophobia, every time we encounter it. But we believe that doing that alone is not enough, that if you want to make a lasting impact on such ideas you have to challenge the system from which they came.

When Marx made his assertion that the material world was paramount, he was rejecting the widely held view that ideas were the fundamental problem in society, a theory that deemed that if only you could rid workers of rotten ideas, superstition and religion, then capitalism would fall.

This notion that "backward" thinking is the main thing that shapes people's lives is still a commonly held view. A government commission on the pay gap between women and men published in 2006 claimed that girls needed their horizons broadened and aspirations raised

(Women and Work Commission, 2006). It doesn't explain that, however great some women's aspirations might be, the very real problem of what to do with your children if you work has to be surmounted.

Marx called this approach "idealism" and he ridiculed it, pointing out that that you cannot overcome drowning by rejecting fear of drowning: "Once upon a time a valiant fellow had the idea that men were drowned in water only because they were possessed with the idea of gravity. If they were to get this notion out of their heads, say by avowing it to be superstition, a religious concept, they would be sublimely proof against any danger from water" (Marx and Engels, *The German Ideology*, p37).

So our material life is what comes first. When a boy or girl is born neither has any sense of "feminine" or "masculine", or of what colours are more appropriate to wear. In fact today's customs only date to the mid-20th century. *The Ladies Home Journal* of June 1918 gave this advice to mothers on babies' clothes: "There has been a great diversity of opinion on the subject, but the generally accepted rule is pink for the boy and blue for the girl. The reason is that pink being a more decided and stronger colour is more suitable for the boy, while blue, which is more delicate and dainty, is prettier for the girl." A newborn baby has no knowledge of Power Rangers or sparkly hair clips, no expectations of a future life. It is the experience of the real world, its customs and habits, which shape our consciousness literally from the day we are born, and boys and girls are treated differently from that moment.

So for example, one classic experiment

Expectation of boys & girls

showing how boy and girl babies are socialised in very different ways was done with a baby that was introduced as a male to half of the study subjects and as a female to the other half. The results showed that, "when the participants thought they were playing with a baby boy, 'he' was offered toys, such as a hammer or rattle, while if the participants thought they were playing with a baby girl, 'she' was offered a doll. But what was most striking was the fact that the participants also touched the baby differently. The baby 'boys' were often bounced...whereas the 'girls' were touched more gently and less vigorously" (Henry Gleitman, Alan Fridlund and Daniel Reisber, *Basic Psychology*, W.W. Norton, 2000).

But you don't need to look up academic journals for examples of how gender differences in babies and children are taken for granted and perpetuated. Check out any children's toyshop. One helpful retailer includes the following tips on its website: "Boys are usually more physically active than girls so boys prefer active, noisy play, and girls choose more social and passive forms of play" (www.toyworldstore.co.uk/student4.asp).

This is not an argument that says that girls and boys are identical. They are clearly not: they do have different bodies, different hormones. But it is society that shapes how the differences are expressed, reinforced and valued. Testosterone need not equal aggression; it could mean enhanced creativity, for example. Even if a child is brought up in a home environment that deliberately rejects gender stereotypes, s/he does not live in a bubble. In the outside world there are increasingly few toys and clothes on offer for children that are genderless.

So if boys grow up to be more at home in rough and tumble games and girls like to host make-believe tea parties, we cannot explain it as simply flowing from timeless instinctual differences, but need to understand how society's expectations, often played out subconsciously, play a role.

In fact what makes humans unique is that so little of how we live is driven by instinct or genetically laid down reflexes, unlike the vast majority of the animal world. While we are part of nature and we live, breathe and die, our capacity for conscious reflective thought makes us distinct among living organisms.

Even the most basic and most essential aspects of our existence, the need to find shelter, food and water, are not driven by instinct. We are not covered by fur or feathers yet we have been able to find a way of living in a huge range of habitats from the Antarctic to the Amazon, an impossibility if we were simply pre-programmed. Not only have humans lived all over the globe, but also the way we fulfil our basic needs today is very different to thousands of years ago. Humans have lived in igloos and tower blocks, caves and space ships; the same cannot be said for the living structures of birds or bears, for example, who live only in specific habitats and whose way of surviving has remained unchanged for millennia.

So when human conscious labour interacts with the environment it doesn't just transform nature: we are transformed in the process too. The numerous changes in how we labour have produced different ways of organising society, and different conceptions about what's natural, different "common senses" about the world.

So for example in the Bronze Age, during the industrial revolution or under advanced capitalism there have been very different ideas about property, the family, the state and religion, unlike the *Flintstones* cartoon which transports the archetypal 1950s family, with its car and trips to the supermarket, to the Stone Age.

In a class society where a minority want to hang on to power, ideas whose effect is to encourage the belief that there is something inevitable about the nature of any given society are fanned and encouraged by the ruling class who benefit most from maintaining the status quo.

Marx said that "the ruling ideas are the ideas of the ruling class". He meant that the ruling class owns the means of reproducing ideas. Today that is the television stations, the newspapers, movie companies or radio networks. Every day we are bombarded by information, some of which overtly aims to direct our thoughts and behaviour, for example, advertising and some of which acts in more subtle ways to shape our opinions.

Does that mean that we are like empty vessels just drinking up all the rubbish they throw at us, absorbing all the "ruling ideas", or do socialists believe that ideas flowing from an unequal society are fixed until such a society is overthrown?

No. Class society is not static and stable and never has been. Ideas and forms of control can be accepted or they can be reisisted. Ideas that have been accepted for many generations can be disposed of in one.

That is why Marx also wrote that the "history of all class societies is the history of class struggle" (Marx and Engels, *The Communist Manifesto*, Bookmarks, 2005).

The contradiction at the heart of capitalism, that a small minority is attempting to maintain control over the vast majority of us, means that there is a constant tension that underlies the apparently smooth surface of society. This sometimes breaks out into open revolt in the shape of strikes and protests, or may just be an invisible but tangible mood of bitterness.

In Britain today we don't need to be held at the barrel of a gun to get up and go to work: we do it voluntarily. We put up with standing on crowded expensive trains. We do our shopping, study for exams, look after our children, wait for hospital treatment. Most of the time it seems that there is no alternative. But when a section of the working class challenge any part of the set up, perhaps ask for a rise, or resist a hospital closure, people start to question lots of other things they had previously accepted. This could be anything, from the power of the media and the state, to perceptions of fellow workers.

Socialists don't want just to wait around and see if the prevailing ideas in society come our way. Women and men are more than just the passive objects of history. We are actively at the forefront of campaigns, protests and day to day challenges to the accepted ideas about every aspect of society, whether it is that "we can't afford to fund the NHS" or that famine in the developing world is merely a "natural disaster". In fact contesting such nonsense is one of the most important jobs for socialists. It is crucial that we challenge rotten ideas wherever they come up. They divide us, make us weaker and lead to us to blaming each other for all that is wrong in the world instead of the real enemy.

★3. It hasn't always been like this

Roots of women's oppression

Society hasn't always looked the way it does now. Even in the 21st century with globalisation and mass air travel there is, amazingly, still a diversity of customs and ways of living in different parts of the world. And until relatively recently there were societies in which the family and women's position were very different to today.

If there is one book which can be said to have revolutionised the way we understand the roots of women's oppression it has to be *The Origin of the Family, Private Property and the State* by Frederick Engels, Marx's great friend and collaborator. It laid out for the first time an analysis of the past, which showed that for the vast part of human history women were not oppressed; there was no state and no private property. It still shapes the debate on the issue to this day, despite the fact that it was written in 1884, not long after Darwin published the groundbreaking *Origin of Species* in 1859.

There have been numerous advances in knowledge about early humans and prehistory since Engels was writing which prove he was mistaken in some assumptions and examples. But his basic premises stand the test of time.

He looked at studies of societies that were believed to have been little touched by the modern world. He saw these as remnants of past, pre-class, societies and believed they could shed light on how even earlier societies were organised. The studies were mainly by white middle class men, sometimes from religious backgrounds, with all the prejudices and preconceptions of their time and class. But they often showed very different relations between women and men than those in capitalist society.

Engels' arguments on this are proved by the evidence, meticulously put together by anthropologist Eleanor Leacock and others. They show there was no domination of men over women among the nomadic hunter-gatherers European settlers encountered in the 17th to 19th centuries (Eleanor Burke Leacock, *Myths of Male Dominance*, Monthly Review, 1982). Leacock tells how Jesuit missionaries, who went out to "civilise" what they regarded as backward societies and to encourage people to live according to contemporary Western values, were shocked to find societies that had no permanent leaders or European family structures and no notions of male authority or female chastity.

Ernestine Friedl has told how, in many such societies, "Individual decisions are possible for both men and women with respect to their daily routines... Men and women alike are free to decide how they will spend each day: whether to go hunting or gathering and with whom" (Ernestine Friedl, *Women and Men, an Anthropologist's View*, Holt, 1975, p17).

Richard Lee has described how even as late as the 1960s, among the !Kung of south west Africa, there was no class or gender hierarchy, with women and men equally involved in communal decision making and free to determine their own individual patterns of life (Richard Lee, *The !Kung San: Men, Women, and Work, in a Foraging Society*, Harvard Univeristy, 1979).

All this evidence proves one thing irrevocably, that there are and have been different ways of living and different ways that men and women have organised society. This in itself is evidence that there is nothing "natural" or preordained about the way we live today.

This small fact has revolutionary implications. For people often argue that women's equality or any sort of socialist society isn't possible because doesn't fit human nature.

The nomadic "hunter-gatherers" Leacock, Friedl and Lee studied were societies who lived in small bands of 40 or so people. That was the way modern human beings lived for more than 90 percent of the 100,000 and more years they have been on the earth. By contrast, the industrial capitalism we live in today has only existed for less than 0.023 percent of that time.

The term hunter-gathering is itself slightly misleading. It suggests the stereotype of "Man the Hunter". But women played a central role in production, since most food came from gathering nuts and berries and from small game hunting which was also done by women. They were able to combine motherhood and productive labour, while men shared in childcare. Big game hunting, which was more generally done by men, was less reliable and more sporadic. These societies did have a division of labour, but, crucially, no different value was placed on the different sorts of work. Engels called it "primitive communism".

So if this sort of egalitarian society was going on

for tens of thousands of years, what changed? Why did women's oppression arise? This is still a question that is hotly debated.

What we know for certain is that around 10,000 years ago groups of people in various parts of the world began to combine hunting and gathering with planting seeds to grow plants and domesticating certain animals.

This necessitated a radical change in people's lives. Hunter-gatherers were usually on the move all through the year, as the band went from place to place seeking wild foodstuffs. The first farmers, by contrast, could remain in the same place, next to their crops and domesticated animals. They could therefore store food and accumulate other elementary forms of wealth. The relations of women and men also began to change.

Hunter-gatherer parents could only have one child at a time, since they had to carry it with them every time they shifted location. The first farmers no longer needed to restrict child births — and since more children eventually meant more people to plant and harvest crops, a high birth rate was to everyone's advantage.

This did not automatically reduce women's position. For many thousands of years — and right down to the mid-20th century in a few parts of the world women were as central to production in agriculture as they had been with hunter-gathering. The instruments of agriculture were light — the hoe and the digging stick. Women continued to be central to decision making, and the family was very different to how we know it today.

But as agriculture became more complex and involved heavier tasks, these tended to devolve on men. Women were impeded from carrying them out through the frequent pregnancies that now became the norm. This began to have a significant impact on women's role in society. There developed a division between the ever more private and increasingly recurring role of reproduction, obviously done by women, and socialised production, increasingly done by men.

One expression of this was an increasing loss of women's personal autonomy. Continuity of production depended on continuity of the male line. Inheritance of property from father to son became important for the first time — and with it monogamy for the woman, to make sure she only had "legitimate" children.

Growing productivity gave rise for the first time to a surplus over and above what was necessary to feed and clothe everybody. Those who controlled this surplus were in a privileged position compared with everyone else. Hierarchies appeared for the first time. And since men had a role in producing the surplus which women did not, it was a minority of men who were at the top of the hierarchy — above the women, but also above most other men.

Once there was a surplus there was also something else that had not existed previously — a motive for war between a society and its neighbours. Again the requirement of child rearing meant women were very, very rarely soldiers — and recipients of the wealth that could come from conquest.

The family as we know it, private property and the state all emerged together.

Women's biology played a role in this, but not in the sense that we were ever innately inferior to men. Rather it was that, for a period of history, the role women played in reproduction precluded the great majority of them from playing a central role in key social developments.

Women became subservient at every level and this became reflected in ideology. For instance, the word family is rooted in the Latin word for domestic slave: "familia" was the total number of slaves belonging to one man.

Engels called this development "the world historic defeat of the female sex". And so it was. Privatised reproduction in the family and social production have shaped, and continue to shape, women's and men's lives in the family to this day.

★ 4. Everything changes so that everything can stay the same

The family has gone through many different transformations over thousands of years, from an extended family where several generations lived under one roof producing everything they needed from candles to bread, to the small nuclear family which is a unit of consumption today.

So why does the family still play such an important role in society in the 21st century, even in parts of the world where heavy ploughs have long been replaced by technology, making physical strength irrelevant, where women can control their fertility and play a large role outside the home?

Marx himself thought the family might disappear during the industrial revolution. The feudal family was torn apart when women and men were forced off their patches of land and sucked into the growing cities to survive by selling their labour power for a wage. Women, and often children, worked long hours in the new mills and factories. Women were seen as particularly suited to work in the coal mines. Half naked because of the heat, they would drag coal wagons down the narrowest shafts. It seemed the family would crumble under the pressures, but it has proved remarkably resilient and adaptable.

Firstly, there was a growing recognition that there

were benefits, both ideological and economic, for the bosses if their workers held on to their family units. For example, if the next generation of workers was going to grow to be healthy and, most importantly, productive, adults then maybe it was better that women didn't give birth in the factories. If men had to financially support a dependent family then maybe they would be more reliable and less likely to cause trouble. Legislation against women's employment in certain jobs and propaganda extolling the virtues of the family served to both persuade and coerce workers to adapt.

But many workers themselves also fought to preserve the family during that period. It became important precisely because their lives had been so brutally ripped apart and seemed at the mercy of the unseen new powers of capital. The family came to represent a place of refuge and solace from the harsh long hours in the new factories that made humans feel like no more than cogs in the system.

At the same time the women of the ruling class were seen as delicate flowers to be protected. They would collapse on the chaise-longue in a swoon with the smelling salts if they felt slighted by not receiving an invite to a ball. If they lifted a finger it was merely to play the pianoforte or stitch some embroidery. For these women the family was about status and producing heirs, and their lives couldn't have been more different from the mass of ordinary women if they had been living in different centuries.

Yet it was the bourgeois family that became upheld and imposed as the model for all society. Designer shopping and the gym may have taken the place of the pianoforte for rich women today but the model remains the ideal, and the difference between their lives and those of most women is still conspicuous.

This convergence of interests between the needs of the ruling class to use the family as a stabilising unit which helps produce successive generations of workers, and the needs of workers to preserve a part of their life which offers love and support, "a haven in a heartless world", is still a feature of the role of the family today.

Of course no one gets married or settles down with a partner saying let's get together and reproduce the next generation of the labour force! Having or being part of a family is seen as a positive element in people's lives. A stable and happy family becomes something to strive for; in a cutthroat world your family can be the one place where you will find unconditional love and support.

Those who have no families because of bereavement, migration or estrangement are objects of compassion. Others have been victims of discrimination, for example lesbians and gay men. Today, however, the advent of civil partnerships, the number of lesbians having children, and the pressure for the law to be changed to make it illegal to bar gay couples from adopting reveal changing attitudes. The longing to be part of a family can be very deep, even among those who have been shunned by the institution in the past.

But sadly for many people hopes of being part of a happy family are brutally dashed. Far from being a haven it can become a very dangerous place.

The shocking figures for domestic violence in the UK tell the story. On average, two women per week are killed by a male partner or ex-partner and nearly half of all female murder victims are killed by a partner or ex-partner. Rape in marriage was legal until overturned in a case as late as 1991. The law was only formally changed in 1994. Current partners (at the time of the attack) were responsible for 45 percent of rapes reported to the British Crime Survey. "Strangers" were only responsible for 8 percent of rape. Children are also far more likely to suffer abuse from adults in their family, including mothers, than they are from a stranger in the street.

It is precisely because the family can be the part of your life from which you are taught to expect so much that when it fails the impact can create a pressure cooker of dashed hopes and bitterness with tragic results.

Economic role of the family

Women and men will scrimp and save, go without, work long hours and make untold sacrifices just to be able to feed their children, or look after an elderly parent or a handicapped relative. Just think how much such care would cost if it were funded by the state. Even the little economic help the welfare state does give is constantly under attack.

New Labour's policies of cutting back on social welfare only serve to increase the economic, physical and psychological burden on individual families, which means women, and working class women above all. On top of the worst childcare in Europe, old people's homes are being closed through lack of funding, nursing care for the elderly is only offered to the severely ill and hospitals kick the sick out faster to meet nebulous targets. If we didn't accept the burden, if simple human decency, love and solidarity didn't exist, society would fall apart.

But just to ensure women don't reject their role, they

are subjected to a never ending ideological onslaught from politicians, the media and advertising eulogising the family and woman's role here as central to her life and fulfilment. The attraction of images of clean, healthy and well-fed children are obvious, less so the campaign to convince us that there is nothing more satisfying than a Flash clean floor and a living room filled with manufactured aroma.

Ideological role of the family

The family is the place where most of us are socialised, where we learn the rules of society, from gender roles to hierarchy. We also learn that when it comes to problems, there is immense pressure to "keep it in the family". For the nuclear family can have a feeling of community within itself but it also serves to atomise people from the wider society.

An infinite number of commodities are marketed as vital to happy family life, from washing machines to personal computers. The message is that all your dreams can come true under one roof. We are encouraged to see problems like poverty or violence as reflecting the personal inadequacies of family members, usually the parents, and not as a reflection of the priorities or shortcomings of society.

The ideological impact of women's perceived role in the family is most significant. Women are still told from an early age that their greatest aspiration is to marry and have a family. We are assured that men's hormones drive them to sleep around and "sow their wild oats", but women's hormones lead them to want to settle with one man, who they may have to ensnare with wile or cunning, or perhaps today be an accomplished pole dancer — all this to fulfil their true role in life, to procreate.

Women who don't fulfil or aspire to this role are seen as in some way unnatural, yet employers are not brought to book for discriminatory policies which put women off having children until they are more financially secure.

The contradiction at the heart of this picture is that the ideology does not fit the reality, and for some women it never did. The vast majority of women today are not full time home makers. The majority of women work, and two thirds of women with children work, compared to less than half 30 years ago. The work they do is essential both to the national economy and to the economic survival of the women themselves, but that doesn't stop the overwhelming ideology that continues to promote their natural attributes as being home making and child loving.

Every day this contradiction between the prevailing ideas and reality is played out in the lives of ordinary women and men. Women work because they need to, yet are made to feel guilty for leaving their children in nursery care. Women who stay at home because they want to spend time with their children, or because their low wages won't cover childcare costs, are deemed scroungers, unless of course they have a wealthy partner who can keep them.

The *Guardian* women's pages regularly feature high flying career women who decide to give it all up to be a full time mum when they have children. But it sticks in the gullet to read of the great fun they have mucking around in the autumn leaves or making chocolate cookies with little Tarquin when the majority of women simply cannot afford to make the decision to stay at home. For most women working is not a lifestyle option but a necessity.

So when the government talks about getting mothers out to work, it doesn't mean the rich women featured in the *Guardian* — it means women who survive on already meagre benefits whom the government sees as a burden it doesn't want to carry in this neoliberal world. As it is, 3.4 million children live in poverty in Britain, and of those 43 percent are in single parent families. If the government really believed in the "family values" it loves to promote then everyone would have choice. Spending time with your children shouldn't be a luxury or an imposition.

The ideology persists because it still works for the system. It keeps women accepting lower pay, flexible working and juggling complicated childcare arrangements. In fact the ideology is needed precisely because this is a contradiction that society wants women to solve themselves, seeing their situation as a personal problem, not one rooted in the way society is organised.

It suits the system for women to still believe they're best at child rearing and all the paraphernalia of housework. Women's oppression is about feeling that things are our fault, our responsibility. It is experienced as an individual; the contradiction is that where we most suffer oppression, in our homes and private lives, is where we are least able to challenge it.

★ 5. What about men?

What about men? It is not society that buys Lads' mags, rapes women or commits domestic violence: it is men. In terms of sex crimes, reported rape figures have risen, in part due to slightly more sympathetic treatment by a majority male police force, but at the same time the ratio of rape convictions to reported rapes has steadily fallen from one in three in 1977 to one in 20 in 2002 (Nicole Westmarland, *Rape Law Reform in England and Wales*, School for Policy Studies, 2004).

There is still a culture that says that women who get drunk, or wear the skimpy clothes featured in every teen magazine, are in some way complicit if they are raped. Men who rape will be confident that they can get away with it. Society simply cannot deal with the problem, for it reflects generations of ideology that says men are naturally sexually promiscuous and can't help themselves.

A recent campaign by the Metropolitan Police is an example. They produced a poster to be pinned up in male toilets of pubs and clubs. It featured a women's torso wearing a pair of pants with a "no entry" sign on. The slogan was, "Have sex with someone who hasn't said yes to it, and the next place you enter could be prison." Not only did the image just encourage a view of women as merely objects, a "place", no more than the sum of her sexual parts, but also it accepted the caricature of men's sexuality. It is saying, "We know how tempting it is for a red blooded man but just think of the punishment."

Hardly a challenge to the prevailing ideology.

This is the sharp end of the experience of some women at the hands of some men. Women's oppression is not a bad smell that wafts through an open window or some ephemeral psychological state. It is articulated through the very real day to day lives of individual women and men and in most cases men are the perpetrators. So are men the enemy? Do they have an interest in maintaining oppression?

Feminist theory would answer yes. It holds that the problem is patriarchy, male dominated society. It is a widely held theory which can be heard down the pub on a Friday night or can be read in esteemed academic journals in the most abstract language, and essentially it boils down to the assertion that "all men are bastards". This flows from a belief that all men are the beneficiaries of our deeply divided society, but it is one that socialists should reject.

It is not only flawed but negates the very real and devastating effects capitalist society has on the mass of humanity, both men and women. It ignores the fact that the majority of men, through their class position, are also denied access to wealth and power in society and so have the potential to find common cause with women.

The statistics help to show why:

* Men die younger than women (the queen sends nine times as many congratulatory telegrams to women reaching 100 as to men).
* The majority of the homeless in Britain are men, as are the majority in prison and mental hospitals.

* Men suffer ill health and more serious illness than women but report it less.
* Young men are more likely to be the victim of violent attack than women.

But one of the most shocking statistics that reveals so much about men's place in modern capitalist society is the suicide figures. In Britain today 75 percent of all suicides are men. Over the past 20 years in the UK the number of women committing suicide has halved, but the number of men committing suicide has increased by 10 percent. It is highest among young men in their late teens and early 20s. Unemployed men are two to three times more at risk of suicide than the general population, and the other peak of male suicide is post-65, after retirement.

This is hardly a picture of a gender at peace with itself, a gender that feels "on top". Men are made to feel worthless if they are not fulfilling the role expected of them, which is to be the provider. What more tragic example can you have of the system turning workers into cogs who have no life outside of work?

But if you are in work, being exploited, being the breadwinner as is expected of you, is it such a great life? Britain has the longest working hours in Europe, and men work their longest hours when they have a partner who has just given birth. "New fathers work the longest hours of all men, working four times as much paid overtime as childless men" (Alexandra Jones and Stephen Bevan, *Where's Daddy? The UK Fathering Deficit*, The Work Foundation, 2003).

An Equal Opportunities Commission survey in January 2007 found that:

* Spending time with the family or finding time for key relationships is the biggest concern in daily life (64 percent) for men and women, ahead of money, health, work and local safety. This concern is felt most strongly by fathers, where 74 percent express this view, compared to 68 percent of mothers.

No wonder men struggle to find time to be a good dad, for instance. One recent reality show portrayed a dad "being mum" for a week. The guy was blown away by the experience. For example, his youngest was always in bed when he got back from work. In one week he saw what he was missing, soul-destroying housework, yes, but spending time with his children, which although stressful was also a joy when he started get to know them. It was tremendously moving watching his realisation that he been conned into believing that being a good father was solely earning money, rather than being there for his kids, and by the end of the week he was determined not to go back to the old way of living.

Even though this was a cheesy reality programme it revealed something true about society, that the roles men are expected to fulfil can break them. They do not just produce the stereotype of fathers who come home and collapse after work, distant, cold and shattered; they also reinforce women taking the prime role with children.

Men's characters are shaped by the earliest taunts not to be a "cry baby" or "mummy's boy", through expectations of physical prowess and sexual conquests to an adulthood of economic success. Their personalities are being crushed to fit into the box that is masculinity under capitalism.

In a crude and opportunistic way the current generation of men's magazines like _Nuts_ and _Zoo_ feed into a sense that this masculinity is under threat by advances that women have made. They declare that they are standing up for old fashioned male values: "We're real men and we're not going to pretend otherwise. We want porn, sport and fast cars and we're not ashamed."

This narrow cliché of manhood says more about how commodities are marketed under capitalism than anything genuine about men's lives, and is hardly a vision of power in society.

★ 6. When society has challenged gender roles

Rosie the Riveter was not a real woman. She was a Norman Rockwell picture on the cover of the US *Saturday Evening Post* in 1943. That image of a women war worker in her overalls eating her sandwich inspired the search for and celebration of hundreds of real life local Rosies working in munitions factories across the US during the Second World War.

The two world wars had a profound impact on every aspect of society in Britain including the lives of women. The needs of the state changed and women were called on to fill the gap in the workforce left by the massive mobilisation of men into the war machine. Government propaganda shifted to convincing women to perform their patriotic duty by going out to do jobs that had previously been the preserve of men.

First World War

The biggest single employer of women before the First World War was domestic service, employing over 1,400,000 women in 1911 (Gail Braybon and Penny Summerfield, *Out of the Cage: Women's Experiences in Two World Wars*, Pandora, 1987). This work involved long hours with few freedoms for women who usually lived in, and so many were attracted to the new jobs on offer through war work. These jobs also had long hours, but with days off and better money. It is no wonder that during this period nearly half a million women left domestic service and the number of women in the industrial workforce grew by 1.5 million.

When the war ended many of these women did not want to go back to the old way of living. They had tasted economic independence and didn't want to lose it. Newspapers denounced women who wouldn't go back to low waged drudgery and quickly forgot their tales of heroic patriotism of women war workers.

The morals of factory women who earned wages, drank in pubs and spent nights out at the music hall were questioned. They also had sex outside of marriage in greater numbers than ever before, and sex manuals were published which sought to educate women about their sexuality and about birth control. All this led to moral panics, a feature of the establishment's disapproval of the behaviour of working class women to this day.

Second World War

Only 16 percent of working women in Britain were married in 1931; by 1943 this had gone up to 43 percent. It was estimated that there were almost 8 million women in paid work in 1943 (Braybon and Summerfield, *Out of the Cage*).

One US study interviewed women as they took up jobs at the start of the war and found that 90 percent said they wanted to give the jobs up when the war was over. However, when the war ended 80 percent declared they wanted to stay in work. Again women had experienced increased financial independence and a loosening of the taboos governing their personal lives. In 1939 just 4.4 percent of babies were born outside marriage; by 1945 this had more than doubled to 9.1 percent (Braybon and Summerfield, *Out of the Cage*).

So after the Second World War ended government propaganda had to shift gear once again. The essential role of mothering was promoted and there was an explosion of books and advice on childcare. *Baby and Childcare* by Benjamin Spock was published in 1946 and sold 40 million copies in six editions, outselling every other book in the history of publishing with the sole exception of the Bible.

In the 1950s such was the dominant ideology that it was common for women to have to give up their jobs because they got married. Yet even then 20 percent of women worked, and as the post-war boom gained momentum so did the need for women workers.

The 1960s

The 1960s were a decade of revolt across the world, for national liberation and against imperialism, for black civil rights in the US and against the US war in Vietnam. The expansion of employment and education drew in women in larger numbers than ever before. Some of these women who found themselves at college and in previously unattainable jobs began to have very different expectations about their lives from previous generations. When they got involved in political action they found the "new" left wanting when it came to understanding women's rights.

This was because when the movements exploded in the US they did so in a vacuum: they had no roots in the socialist tradition of the past that had understood women's oppression. The 1950s had seen the left smashed by McCarthyism, and the brutal experience of Stalinism in the Soviet Union cast a long shadow. The thread of the socialist tradition had been broken. So women began to organise on their own.

In contrast in Britain socialist politics were central to the women's movement, so early demands and struggles concentrated on the very real problems faced by working class women, such as equal pay and childcare.

The transformation in attitudes to personal morality was dramatic. The contraceptive pill became widely available and abortion was made legal with the 1967 Act so sex could be separated from unwanted pregnancy for the first time. Homosexuality was legalised and divorce laws were liberalised. Everyone wasn't rolling around naked in mud at music festivals, as popular memory would imply, but undeniably a great cloud of guilt and pain was lifted from the experience of sex for millions of women and men.

As the 1970s wore on, the movements went into decline, and the struggle for women's liberation was no exception. In the end it fragmented into bitter factions, between those who wanted to organise as women, those who wanted to involve men in the struggle, between lesbians and straight women (who were accused by the former of sleeping with the enemy), and a myriad other divisions.

The women's liberation movement had raised the banner of equality and liberation, but didn't have the means, the politics or the organisation to win it for the mass of women.

★ 7. Women and Class

What sort of equality are we fighting for? Equality with whom? There is a big difference between winning equality with a man who is a managing director of a multinational company and, say, a hospital porter. Any struggle that aims only for equality between women and men leaves the deepest division in society intact, that of class.

The Institute for Public Policy Research shows that the richest 10 percent in Britain own 54 percent of national wealth, up from 47 percent under John Major's Tory government. Those at the very top, the richest 1 percent, have seen their share of wealth rise even faster, from 17 percent to 23 percent over roughly the same period. For comparison, the bottom 50 percent now own only 7 percent of Britain's resources.

But in Marxist terms class is not defined just by wealth nor is it defined by what people think about their position. It's not a box we allocate people to; it's not a static category; instead it's about an objective social relationship in the system: if you are exploited or the exploiter, if you have control or no control, if you live off the labour of others or you have to sell your labour to survive.

The trappings of class, your accent or lifestyle, all flow from this fundamental relationship, and even these change. Today some manual workers may wear designer clothes and eat in restaurants or have foreign holidays; 50 years ago such lifestyles would only have been the preserve of a small privileged elite in society.

But these are superficial changes. The fundamental relationship still remains. The minority at the top of society is still exploiting the vast majority of us. Workers do everything. Without workers trains, buses and tubes wouldn't run, buildings wouldn't get built, roads mended, the sick cared for, or children taught.

For socialists the working class is a unique social force. First, it has potentially great economic power, because if workers decide to stop work society can't function, whereas if bosses like Richard Branson take a year off, no one notices. Secondly the working class is a collective force. Capitalism pushes us apart with divisions like racism and sexism but it also has to push us together, all the better to exploit us. Workers have to cooperate in huge workplaces just to produce every day, and the only way to defend their interests is to organise together.

If a worker for British Airways or a large hospital wants a pay rise, he or she can't just approach the managing director and ask for one. Instead workers, men and women, have to approach management en masse through their collective organisations. This means workers are forced to overcome the divisions among themselves if they are to have a strong side. No other section of society has such an inherent interest in challenging and overcoming division.

So socialists don't see the working class as the vehicle for change because workers are necessarily less prejudiced and more cuddly and liberal right now, but because history shows that the pressure for unity in the class creates the conditions for prejudices to be overcome.

Today women are about half that workforce. The majority, 70 percent, work, even those with children — 68 percent of women (www.statistics.gov.uk).

Is this not just another burden on women? The crucial difference is that their role in the workforce takes women out of the atomised drudgery of the home into social production, to a place where women are not just victims but can become class fighters. And women workers have shown their willingness to go into battle against the system time after time.

Being part of the social force that has the potential to challenge capitalism is central to prospects of liberation. This is not about looking to someone else to liberate us; it's about women organising where we are most powerful.

★ 8. Women's lives today

There is a deep contradiction in the lives of women today, for on the one hand there have been huge advances for women in the last 100 years, while on the other we still face discrimination throughout society and are far from reaching equality in Britain or in fact anywhere across the globe.

Our lives have been transformed in ways that would have been unthinkable in our grandmothers' time. They suffered backbreaking housework, lack of access to education, a crushing morality on all aspects of their personal lives, unreliable or unsafe contraception, illegal abortion and whole sections of employment barred to them.

My granny was born in Ireland in 1898, always wore her "pinny", sewed, mended and knitted clothes, baked and cooked every meal from scratch and boil-washed the laundry before putting it through a hand wringer. In contrast all of her granddaughters work full time outside the home, use every bit of new technology to make housework as easy as possible and have been known to eat food that has been preprepared.

If in just two generations of one family women's lives have become unrecognisable, in wider society in Britain the changes are truly remarkable. Having won the vote for women over 30 in 1918 and then universal suffrage for all women and men in 1928 women are now potentially part of all the political structures in British society: they can become MPs, peers (though the upper house is still called the House of Lords); they can sit on juries, become lawyers, barristers and judges. In terms of employment it is illegal to bar women from particular jobs. It is also illegal to pay women less than men for the same job.

The difference in public morality and its impact on our personal lives is extraordinary. Safe and reliable contraception is widely available to women whatever their martial status, abortion is legal, divorce possible, and having children outside of marriage and living with a partner without marrying are commonplace.

These gains are real but there is still a long way to go.

Equal pay

Equal pay may be enshrined in the law but women on average earn 18 percent less than men. A 2006 government commission on women and work showed that women leave college with the same qualifications as young men, or better, but showed that it only takes five years for the pay gap to kick in (Women and Work Commission, 2006).

The scandal of low pay in general and the even lower pay average for women workers in particular has to be laid at the door of the bosses who pay the wages. But instead of berating them and imposing statutory measures, for instance pay reviews that would monitor pay differences, to uphold the law, the commission tried to win them by assuring them that "gender equality is good for UK business".

The commission went on to state that "some of us believe that the voluntary approach is the best way forward. Some stakeholders feel the same, for instance the CBI feel that mandatory pay reviews would represent an excessive burden, "out of proportion to the problem and out of tune with the current deregulatory climate".

So the government agrees with big business that legally enforcing equal pay legislation would be an imposition, that the problem is not that important, and given that New Labour doesn't control business in any other way, to do it over women's pay would be an anomaly!

But of course without enforcing legislation employers will continue to pay poverty wages if they can get away with it. When the Equal Pay Act was first passed in May 1970 bosses were given five years grace to make changes before it came into force in 1975. They didn't budge then, and 36 years on there is still a pay gap. Why would bosses suddenly submit now without being forced to?

The New Labour government likes to boast that it helps low paid workers through benefits. In particular Gordon Brown often cites the introduction of his Working Tax Credit as a great initiative for supporting families. But this is not support for low paid workers: it is a way for the state to subsidise employers who pay less than a living wage. Bosses are the real scroungers.

The pay situation is even worse for women who work part time. They earn 32 percent less than the hourly earnings of women who work full time and an astonishing 41 percent less than men who work full time. The majority of part time workers are women, because those are often the only jobs that they can get to fit round the demands of bringing up children.

Childcare

Publicly funded childcare in Britain is widely acknowl-
edged to be the worst in Europe. The government
regularly launches initiatives to "encourage" women
with children to go out to work, generally in the form of
threatening to withdraw benefits from already vulner-
able women. Instead the one initiative that would enable
women to make that choice, providing a national net-
work of high quality free or at least affordable nurseries
for working parents, is rejected.

Today the typical average cost of a full time nursery place for a child under two is £141 per week, but
prices can vary around this quite dramatically. In some
areas parents can expect to pay closer to £200 per week,
and some nurseries charge as much as £350 a week
(www.childcaretrust.org.uk). At present lone parents
in Britain are on average contributing around 70 percent of childcare costs privately, in comparison to other
European nations such as Scandinavia where the average
contribution is closer to 30 percent with the rest being
subsidised.

No wonder many low paid women simply can't
afford to work, as the costs of having their child looked
after are greater than their wage.

Wealthy professional women will get a nanny, sometimes even two, and will rarely be criticised for neglect.
Instead they will be praised for being "superwomen".
The fact is the minority of women who do break through
the glass ceiling manage only because they rely on an
army of other women who don't.

But it is still only a few who break through. The higher
up in society you look in terms of political and economic

power, the fewer women you see. There are only three women managing directors of top FTSE 100 companies, only 19 percent of MPs are women and in the judiciary there is only one woman appeal judge. Only a quarter of top managers in the civil service are women and only one in ten senior police officers (*Sex and Power: Who Runs Britain*, Equal Opportunities Commission, 2006/2007).

Women are 50 percent of the population, if there was anything resembling gender equality in place in Britain today, then women would do around half of most jobs throughout society earning the same as men.

★ 9. Raunch culture

Children's clothes sport the Playboy bunny logo, T-shirts for eight year olds feature hands over non-existent breasts, lap dancing clubs are big business and soft porn has become mainstream. Self-help books promise you'll "Make Love Like a Porn Star", and classes to learn how to strip proclaim that "fan dancing is life affirming". This isn't sexism, we are told. Apparently being a sex object in the 21st century is ironic, fun and empowering, and we should celebrate it for fear of being denounced as a prude.

Everyone can join in. In 2006 Loughborough University students union hosted the Brat Pack Tour (courtesy of *Nuts* magazine) where punters were promised the chance to meet the magazine's models. Loughborough students union also invited the "High Street Honeys" Tour, organised by the Lads' magazine *FHM*. The tour aims to "discover" ordinary women from the high street to be topless models in the magazine. Not content with parading half naked *FHM* models around, women students were invited to strip off to see if they were "high street honey" material. The posters advertising the tour portrayed the usual topless "girl on girl" poses with the catchline "Want to know how far they've really gone with one another?" At York University students union they even have their very own "Pole Exercise" club whose logo is a naked women sliding down a pole.

Is a rejection of all this just a case of an older

generation of women shaking their heads in disapproval at the clothes and behaviour of the younger generation? No, young women, and young men across the country, particularly in colleges and student unions, have organised to stop lap dancing clubs targeting students, and hold political meetings to debate issues of women's oppression and sexuality thrown up by the growth of raunch culture.

This isn't just about the buying and selling of porn, which has obviously mushroomed with the impact of the internet, but about what some women are calling the "pornification" of popular culture. The television schedules are crammed with programmes on sex, some of which purport to be serious documentaries, some of which don't even pretend to be anything more than an excuse to broadcast images of women's bodies.

So what's new about this? Haven't women been seen as sex objects for a long time, especially in advertising to sell anything from tyres to quick dry concrete? Yes, but the difference today is that this is being sold to women as empowering, as a way to let go of their inhibitions, as a way of being liberated about their sexuality, as if making love like someone who is faking it for the cameras to make a living is the recipe for a great sex life.

Sex is a uniquely valuable currency. It is an intrinsic part of being human, and can be life affirming and amazing, provoking the most intense emotions. Our sexuality feels so private, such an intimate part of our personality, that if we can't express ourselves, or if we are unhappy about it, it can have a devastating impact. Many lesbians and gay men will testify to the effects of being told that your natural feelings are "perverted" or "unacceptable".

But capitalism, by turning sex into a commodity, makes parts of our humanity alien to us and messes with our potential to have a fulfilling sexuality. It becomes something to be achieved, to succeed at, to work at. It is shaped by the world around us and affects even the most basic emotions about how we feel about our bodies.

Commercial sex, whether it is porn or lap dancing, is like fast food. It is a horrible, soulless version of something good which capitalism sells back to us after stripping us of the time and well-being which would allow us enjoyment of the real thing. Far from being liberating, raunch culture is a straitjacket, a narrow and clichéd view of what society defines as sexy that we are literally being squeezed into. The only way to be sexy is to act and look like a porn star, we're being told. It is sexual liberation through the prism of capitalism.

This is not about being prudish. Nor is it calling for censorship. Giving the state power to control what we see and read, to curtail sexual images or publications, is not the way forward. Who decides what's perverted? The judges and politicians? They would prosecute what they think is perverted and have done, so gay sex shops and gay publications have always been targeted in the past.

As it is, magazines aimed at straight men are filled with images of women pretending to have sex with each other and are seen as perfectly acceptable for display on every street corner, while lesbians who enjoy real sex with each other in private without "cameras, lights, action" and, most importantly, the exchange of cash, are still not fully accepted and are virtually invisible in society.

Far from calling for sex to be hidden and shameful,

socialists campaign for more openness in society. For young people sex as a commodity is glaring from every newsstand but education about sex and relationships in many schools is still woefully inadequate. In fact school students petitioned Number 10 Downing Street in 2006 demanding decent education in their schools. Sex education in schools should be more explicit and sympathetic, so that young people are better equipped to deal with the period in their lives when they are coming to terms with and exploring their sexual feelings.

The sexual openness won in the struggles of the 1960s and 1970s was hard fought for and we want to defend and extend it. We don't want to go back to the 1950s. But capitalism will assimilate anything, even resistance, and turn it into a commodity, You can buy trainers with peace signs on, and sexual openness is being sold back to us as push-up bras and glorified strip clubs.

Bound up with this is an ever increasing obsession about women's appearance that has broken new boundaries. When I was growing up as a teenager in the 1970s reading *Jackie* magazine, it was made clear that your appearance as a young woman was paramount. Weekly articles would explain how to apply complicated shading on cheekbones and eyelids with make up. Now even all that is not enough. Cosmetic surgery is becoming mainstream. One cosmetic surgery company quotes on its website that plastic surgery "is no longer just for the rich and famous, as more and more everyday people opt for surgery *to improve their lives*" (my emphasis — www. cosmeticsurgeryconsultants.co.uk).

But this is not just about "people"; it's about women and how much their sense of confidence and self-worth is distorted by society's expectations of their appearance. Of the 28,921 procedures carried out last year 26,469 (92 percent) were performed on women, and the most popular operation is breast "enhancement". A BBC radio survey reported that 50 percent of women questioned said they would consider plastic surgery (www.bbc.co.uk, February 2007). In any other culture this would be denounced as mutilation; in ours it is just another consumer choice.

The latest debate over skeletal models and the almost mythical size zero is also part of this obsession with women's appearance. Size zero is a US clothes size which is the equivalent of a UK size four. The name is appropriate, as any women of average height would have to fade away to virtually nothing to achieve it. But it has become the aspirational size in the fashion industry, and is now available in Britain in shops like Top Shop and Gap.

Models in Britain are now on average six clothes sizes smaller than the average women. Several models have died in the last 12 months of problems relating to malnutrition. But even these dangerously thin women will find that their photos have been touched up after the photo shoot, legs made a bit longer, breasts a bit larger. The untouched up pictures of the famous that crowd the front pages of magazines like *Heat* feature "flabby" tummies one week and bony shoulders the next. If wealthy celebrities with dieticians and personal trainers can't be the perfect shape, what hope is there for the rest of us?

Is this what we've come to? The freedom to gyrate round a pole to titillate men, the freedom to inject poison into our faces to paralyse muscles so wrinkles don't show, or to slice our breasts open and insert silicon bags to make them look bigger?

This isn't about having a prescription of "accept-able" and "unacceptable" behaviour; it's about having a vision of real sexual liberation, with real openness and choice for everyone.

★ 10. How does change come?

How are things ever going to change?

All the gains that ordinary people have made in the past have come through struggle. This is true of everything from having paid holidays to winning the right to vote. But when life chugs along from one workday to the next, when all you think about is how long it is till the weekend or your next holiday, it is hard to envisage what it would be like if we turned the world upside down.

Imagine if we were able to take control of our lives, from the daily details to the big global questions like war, climate change and famine. Such momentous struggles have taken place in the past and they offer an inspiring vision of the potential for changing society and in the process ourselves.

The sense of exhilaration and new possibilities leaps off the page when you read accounts both of great historic events like the Paris Commune or the Spanish Civil War, and of disputes like the Great Miners' Strike in Britain in 1984-85. Then, despite all the strikers being men, women played a decisive role. Ordinary people grow in stature during such events; years of hard grind and being told they're worthless are brushed aside in days or weeks of struggle.

Struggle on a mass scale not only makes a specific challenge to the economic power of the ruling class, but also opens up the possibility for new ideas and new ways of organising to break out on a scale unimagined in the humdrum routine of the past.

In every great struggle of the past women have come to the forefront, and when they do they change their own ideas about what they are capable of, of what the possibilities are. But also by being a part of the struggle alongside women, men's ideas and preconceptions about women change, which in turn has the very real effect of making our side stronger and more united and more able to make further advances. Nothing changes ideas on a mass scale like the real lived experience of struggle.

The most powerful example of such an experience of a mass movement for change is the Russian Revolution of 1917.

Russian Revolution

The Russian Revolution was a spectacular explosion of popular democracy and led to a blossoming of ordinary people's potential. Hundreds of thousands of poor workers and peasants who had been illiterate, and felt that their brutal lives were destined by an unchangeable god, learned to read, write, got involved in the big debates of the day and took part in taking control of their own lives.

The question of women's liberation was central to the revolution. Women who lived in the most oppressed conditions, where in large areas it was even legal for wives to be whipped, flooded into the revolutionary movement. One of the leaders of the revolution, Leon Trotsky, wrote movingly about the sheer brutality of women's lives, writing that "the revolution made a heroic effort to destroy the so called family hearth — that archaic, stuffy, and stagnant institution in which the women of the toiling classes perform galley labour from childhood till death" (Leon Trotsky, *Women and the Family*, Pathfinder, 1974).

The Bolsheviks knew that in order to enable women to be able to play an active part in the political life of the revolution they would have to free them from this isolating burden. Alexandra Kollontai led the Zhenotdel, the department set up to take special measures to get women involved. All over this vast country ravaged by war and famine the Bolsheviks organised literacy programmes, state nurseries and laundries.

"New political, civic, economic and family codes aimed to wipe away centuries old inequalities with one stroke. The new government granted women the right to vote, passed divorce and civil laws which made marriage a voluntary relationship, eliminated the distinction between legitimate and illegitimate children, enacted employment rights for women equal to those for men, gave women equal pay and introduced paid maternity leave" (Tony Cliff, *Class Struggle and Women's Liberation*, Bookmarks, 1984). Russia was also the first country in the world to legalise abortion.

But all the hopes and potential of the revolution could not stand up to the immense pressure from its enemies, and not only were many of the plans not fulfilled but eventually the revolution itself could not survive. The fate of women is always tied to the strength of our side. By the late 1920s the rise of Stalinism marked the end of both the revolution and the gains women had made.

Trotsky opposed Stalin and was exiled from Russia. He wrote that one of the ways he could tell that the revolutionary ideals for which he and the Bolsheviks had fought were on the retreat was what was happening to the lives of women. He noted that women were going back to doing their own washing instead of using the social laundries which had deteriorated so much that they "tear and steal linen more than they wash it". This was a man who had led the Red Army against the invading imperialist powers of the world, a man who had been the leader of the Petrograd Soviet, which had been at the heart of workers' power in the new state. Yet he understand how significant these apparently small changes in the daily lives of women were in revealing the true nature of the society that was replacing the hopes of the revolution.

All this was half a century before the Women's Liberation Movement of the 1960s when Betty Friedan famously wrote about the predicament of women as the "problem that had no name". This predicament did have a name, women's oppression, and women and men had already been fighting to challenge it for several generations.

★ 11. A Vision of the Possible

The struggle continues today and every day. All over the country people resist, in a multitude of different ways, to attacks on their rights, living conditions and local communities. Socialists don't sit back and wait for revolutionary change but get involved in every one of these struggles, however small.

Each is important both for the immediate improvements it might win — a nursery that stays open, a pay rise won — but also for the unity it forges on our side and for the impact it has on our attitudes to the world. If we can stop a hospital ward closing or stop a fellow worker being bullied, then maybe we can challenge the wider priorities of society that created these conditions.

The fight for women's liberation is inextricably linked with the struggles of the whole working class. Women have made the greatest gains when the whole of our side is confident and winning, and we have faced the worst conditions when workers are on the retreat.

Ultimately women's issues are class issues, from abortion and fertility rights to breast cancer treatment. If we only organise as women we miss out on the solidarity and strength of the rest of our class. When abortion rights have come under attack in the past some activists organised women-only marches, but the biggest demo ever to defend abortion rights was in 1979 when 80,000 marched. The demo was organised by the TUC and involved men and women trade unionists. Its size and defiance ensured that the anti-abortion bigots were resolutely defeated.

The fact that discrimination is still rampant today reflects the fact that capitalism, class society, is still with us. The changes we have won, though hugely welcome, have left the system that created women's oppression in the first place still intact.

Women's oppression is fundamental to class society; the divisions it sows in the working class have played a role in maintaining the rule of the minority for thousands of years. Trotsky said of women's oppression that it was so deeply rooted that "a heavy going plough is needed to uproot the heaviest clods of earth".

That deep going plough is a revolution, a socialist revolution. A revolution is nothing if it is not a carnival of the oppressed, a chance for all of us to blossom as individuals, to take control of our lives, for all to reach their full potential.

Frederick Engels was asked what relations between men and women would be like after such a revolution. He wrote:

"That will be answered when a new generation has grown up: a generation of men who never in their lives have known what it is to buy a woman's surrender with money or any other social instrument of power; a generation of women who have never known what it is to give themselves to a man from any other considerations than real love, or to refuse to give themselves to their lover from fear of the economic consequences. When these people are in the world, they will care precious little what anybody today thinks they ought to do; they will make their own practice and their corresponding public opinion about the practice of each individual — and that will be the end of it."

That a middle aged man from the Victorian age can speak so poignantly to us in our times, about problems that seem so modern, is a testimony to the fact that he was also a revolutionary, a socialist, and he wanted to turn society upside down. He saw beyond how the world was to how it could be. He had a vision of the possible, a society where the whole of humanity can be free from exploitation and oppression.

We are still fighting for such a society today.

FURTHER READING

The best place to start is *Sex, Class and Socialism* by Lindsey German (Bookmarks, 1998). For an introduction to Marx's approach read *The Revolutionary Ideas of Karl Marx* by Alex Callinicos (Bookmarks, 2004). Engels' *The Origin of the Family, Private Property and the State* (Pathfinder, 1972) remains the classic Marxist approach to the origins of women's oppression, and the essay by Chris Harman in *The Revolutionary Ideas of Frederick Engels*, International Socialism special issue 65 (1995), defends Engels' approach while explaining some minor mistakes.

Some of Alexandra Kollontai's writings are gathered together in the pamphlet *On Women's Liberation* (Bookmarks, 1998) and some of Trotsky's writings on women in *Women and the Family*, (Pathfinder, 1974). A personal account of the US women's movement can be found in Sara Evans' *Personal Politics* (Vintage, 1980) while *Female Chauvinist Pigs* by Ariel Levy is a searing indictment of the new "raunch culture" (Pocket books, 2006).

Finally, a fantastic resource is the Women's Library at London Metropolitan University which has a collection of books and original magazines, pamphlets and newsletters on the history of women's struggles, their website is: www.thewomenslibrary.ac.uk

566283